POEMS OF THE MACABRE

Laura Shenton

POEMS OF THE MACABRE

Laura Shenton

Iridescent Toad Publishing

Iridescent Toad Publishing.

©Laura Shenton 2023
All rights reserved.

Laura Shenton asserts the moral right to be identified as the author of this work.

No part of this publication may be reproduced, stored or transmitted in any form or by any means, electronic, mechanical, photocopying, recording, scanning, or otherwise without written permission from the publisher. It is illegal to copy this book, post it to a website, or distribute it by any other means without permission.

All cover images used under a commercial license.

First edition. ISBN 978-1-9163478-1-6

Whispers in the Gloom

Whispers in the gloom,
Unseen hands that linger.
In the corners they gather,
Malevolence growing ever stronger.

Tainted Reflection

In the mirror's tainted gaze,
A distorted image plays.
Eyes that pierce the soul,
A reflection, consuming whole.

Mourning Bells

Mourning bells toll despair,
Ringing aloud within the air.
A requiem for lost souls,
Eternally bound, and taken whole.

Dance of the Shadows

Beneath the moon's pallid glow,
Shadows dance, an explicit show.
In their embrace, darkness reigns,
Hinting at secrets, but candour restrained.

The Forgotten Path

A path forgotten by time,
Twisted, overgrown, sublime.
Footsteps echo in empty air,
The wandering souls, unaware.

Cobwebbed Matrix

Cobwebbed matrix, puzzles bind,
Elusive tales of a private kind.
Silken threads of deceit and woe,
Entangled hearts, alone below.

Night's Embrace

Night's embrace, a velvet touch,
Enveloping all with a sinister clutch.
Moonlight stalks the truths untold,
Unveiling darkness, the enigma unfolds.

Crimson Dusk

Crimson dusk, a bloodied sky,
Bleeding hues, as daylight dies.
The world is cloaked in eerie red,
An unnerving scene, where nightmares tread.

Drowning in Dreams

Drowning in dreams, a murky abyss,
Twisted visions, a sleepwalker's tryst.
Horrors entwined in slumber's grasp,
Reality's tendrils, they gently unclasp.

The Withered Rose

The withered rose, once vibrant and alive,
Now a relic, where beauty cannot thrive.
Petals wilted, colours turned to dust,
Love's memory, buried beneath rust.

Veiled Desires

Veiled desires, forbidden and corrupt,
Lurking in souls, their manner abrupt.
Passions suppressed, yearning to break free,
Unleashing chaos, a tempestuous spree.

The Cursed Portrait

Within the cursed portrait's frame,
Is a captured soul, forever retained.
Eyes that follow, a smile that taunts,
A disturbing presence that forever haunts.

In the Marrow's Grasp

In the marrow's grasp, a chilling hold,
Frozen still, a life untold.
Beneath fragile skin, secrets reside,
Unearthed by time, but never by pride.

The Siren's Spell

Beware the siren's alluring spell,
Her voice, a relentless melody to quell.
She lures you into the depths unknown,
Where disturbance thrives and dreams are thrown.

The Puppeteer's Dance

Strings pulled by the puppeteer's hand,
Dancing marionettes, at his command.
Their painted smiles conceal despair,
Trapped in a performance, so unfair.

Midnight's Symphony

Midnight's symphony, a dissonant score,
Playing through the night, forevermore.
Notes of sorrow, notes of dread,
Melodies woven from souls long dead.

Eternity's Embrace

In eternity's embrace, spirits collide,
Unseen forces, bound by fate, coincide.
Time's relentless march, an unending reign,
Condemning souls to eternal pain.

Echoes of the Crypt

Echoes of the crypt, whispers arise,
Ghosts of the past, with vacant eyes.
Their voices linger, in cold, damp air,
Recounting tales with an absent glare.

Memento Mori

Memento mori, a reminder of death,
A macabre truth, stealing every breath.
In life's fleeting moments, we're mere pawns,
Bound by mortality's inevitable dawn.

Tenebrous Veil

Behind the tenebrous veil, secrets reside,
A realm of query, where fears abide.
Shrouded in mystery, the unseen awaits,
A world concealed beyond the gates.

The Raven's Lament

The raven's lament, an ode to the fallen,
In sombre notes, their memories woven.
The song, a canvas of unyielding woe,
A sentiment where hope fails to grow.

The Labyrinth's Maze

Embedded within the labyrinth's maze,
A twisted path, where uncertainty plays.
Confusing corridors, leading astray,
Spiralling deeper, towards disarray.

Vesper's Toll

Vesper's toll, a requiem for the night,
Echoing through the hallowed site.
Cheerless melodies, ghosts unite,
In the clutches, taking flight.

Silent Tombstones

Silent tombstones, etched with names,
Memories eternally locked in frames.
Who they were, only some may know,
With time, the mystery will grow.

The Haunted Hour

The haunted hour, when midnight strikes,
Ghouls awaken, in spectral hikes.
The line between the worlds is thin,
As cries of yearning dwell within.

The Dusk's Demise

With dusk's demise, the spectres creep,
Through hidden crevices, each presence seeps.
In the fading light, they dance and sway,
Enchanting, in their wicked ballet.

The Moth's Lament

The moth's lament, wings ablaze,
Drawn to the flame, in a fiery haze.
A fatal attraction, desire undone,
A tragic end, forever to stun.

Whispers of the Wind

Whispers of the wind, eerie and cold,
Tales of woe, long untold.
Carrying words from distant lands,
Invisible messengers, in ghostly strands.

Withered Roots

Beneath the withered roots, agony dwells,
A hidden realm, where longing swells.
Tangled veins, entwined with dread,
Nourishing the earth, with tears long shed.

Dance of the Banshee

In the moonlit glade: the banshee's dance,
Beseeching cries, a spectral trance.
Her voice, a shriek, piercing the night,
Summoning souls lost in their plight.

The Pendulum's Swing

The pendulum swings, time's cruel decree,
Tick by tick, it claims its fee.
Every moment, a step towards the end,
Relentless foe, it's not a friend.

Haunted Eyes

Haunted eyes, windows to the soul,
Revealing tales as black as coal.
Glimpses of anguish, flickers of pain,
An insight into a tortured reign.

Funeral March

In the funeral march's sombre sway,
Mourning souls, draped in dismay.
A weight of loss, resonating deep,
In death's embrace, they forever sleep.

The Cloak of Illusion

Behind the cloak of illusion, shadows lie,
Concealing truths, shrouded in cries.
Reality's murmurs, a ghostly charade,
Masking the horrors, in cover they fade.

Midnight's Shroud

Midnight's shroud, a cloak of black,
A time for loners, not a pack.
Misaligned motives, how they strive,
When under cover, nightmares thrive.

Spectral Wail

A spectral wail, through the mist it cries,
Piercing the air, where sorrow lies.
Taunting in halls of disrepair,
Bold and festering in the stagnant air.

The Serpent's Kiss

Beware the serpent's venomous kiss,
A treacherous lure, a deceiving bliss.
Its fangs, a portal to the abyss,
Where innocence dies, and evil persists.

Dance of the Macabre

In the dance of the macabre, souls entwine,
A waltz of grief, a symphony malign.
Skeletons twirl with ethereal grace,
An elegant spectacle in this sombre space.

Bleak Solitude

Bleak solitude, an empty room,
Where phantoms dwell in eternal gloom.
Emotion swells in vacant halls,
Resonating woe, as dusk befalls.

The Spider's Web

Within the spider's web, dreams are ensnared,
Frail hopes tangled, forever impaired.
Within silken threads of beauty spun,
A weaving of hurt, from which no one can run.

Moonlit Cemetery

In the moonlit cemetery, spirits roam,
Ghosts yearn intensely, buried in stone.
Names erased by time, memories fade,
Yet their presence lingers, in the hallowed glade.

The Harbinger's Call

The harbinger's call, a prophecy of fear,
Traversing aloud, there's no peace here.
An omen of doom, a prelude to dread,
A message most clear, for the living and dead.

Whispers of the Grave

Whispers of the grave, carried by the wind,
Voices of the departed never rescind.
Throughout night and day, their messages blend,
Eternal voices never to end.

Mourning Veil

A mourning veil, draped in misery's guise,
Concealing tears and the heart's demise.
A widow's reflection, a weighted dirge,
Veiling pain, emotions submerged.

Ghostly Embrace

In a ghostly embrace, souls entwine,
Ethereal lovers, forever aligned.
Bound by love in the realm of the deceased,
Their passion's flame, eternally unleashed.

The Abandoned Doll

The abandoned doll, porcelain and frail,
A silent witness to a tragic tale.
Lifeless eyes hauntingly stare,
Her broken heart beyond repair.

The Forsaken Manor

Within the forsaken manor, foreboding thrives,
Carried by phantoms, their souls still alive.
Walls hold memories of a twisted past,
An uncomfortable saga, destined to last.

Funeral Elegy

A funeral elegy, loss' lament,
A hymn for the departed, as souls are sent.
Through tear-stained verses, sorrow unfurls,
An ode to the lost, in the underworld.

The Quiet Chapel

In the quiet chapel, spirits dwell,
Echoing prayers, a solemn spell.
Stained glass windows, a kaleidoscope of pain,
A sanctuary of souls, forever chained.

Forgotten Lullaby

A forgotten lullaby, a chilling refrain,
Shared by ghosts, a melancholic strain.
A mother's song, pleading with the night,
Resonating anguish, until morning's light.

Chalice of Poison

In the chalice of poison, uncertainty brews,
A potent elixir, a malicious ooze.
Could this be a settling of scores?
Into oblivion, it slowly absorbs.

The Banshee's Cry

The banshee's cry, a wailing plea,
Piercing the sky with chilling decree.
Her voice, a harbinger of impending doom,
Announcing tragedy, to the world's gloom.

The Gargoyle's Gaze

Beneath the gargoyle's gaze, the sinister thrives,
Eyes of stone, where malevolence resides.
A sentinel perched upon haunted spires,
Guarding a realm, fuelling grim desires.

Wicked Labyrinth

Within the wicked labyrinth, souls desperately roam,
Trapped in a web, they can't get home.
Twisted corridors, endless and obscure,
Where bad dreams linger, forever impure.

The Mourner's Tear

The mourner's tear, a crystalline call,
In grief's embrace, it frigidly falls.
A testament to loss, a heartbreak profound,
A single tear, a world unbound.

Elegy of the Moon

Elegy of the moon, a mournful tune,
Its presence reflecting in lavish bloom.
Serenaded ghosts, the lost souls unite,
Embracing the macabre, in their path of flight.

www.ingramcontent.com/pod-product-compliance
Lightning Source LLC
Chambersburg PA
CBHW030044100526
44590CB00011B/333